THE CHANGING LIVES OF WOMEN TRAVELLERS

WOMEN'S STUDIES MONOGRAPH SERIES VOL. 4

Irene Norman

Series Editor: Patricia Daniel

University of Wales, Bangor
2002

© Irene Norman, 2002

All rights reserved. No part of this book may be reproduced, stored in a retrieval system or transmitted, in any form or by any means, electronic, mechanical, photocopying, recording or otherwise, without clearance from the Department of Lifelong Learning, University of Wales, Bangor, Dean Street, Bangor.

ISBN 1-84220-034-8

Cover photograph *'Ida Smith'* still produced from the video *Always Moving On* courtesy of Barrie Law, Romany Gypsy Photographs, 121 York Road, Strensall, York YO32 5ZG.

Published by the Department of Lifelong Learning, University of Wales, Bangor, Gwynedd
Printed by WO Jones Printers, Ffordd yr Efail, Llangefni, Ynys Môn

University of Wales, Bangor • Women's Studies Monograph Series
The Changing Lives of Women Travellers • Irene Norman

CONTENTS

Introduction: Finding a Voice
Patricia Daniel   **2**

The Changing Lives of Women Travellers
Irene Norman

    1. The Traveller Woman in Context:
       An Overview   **6**

    2. Research Methodology   **12**

    3. The Fieldwork Experience   **18**

    4. Mothers and Daughters   **31**

    5. Conclusion   **37**

         Acknowledgements   **40**

         Glossary   **40**

         Bibliography   **41**

INTRODUCTION

Finding a Voice

The first cohort of students on the postgraduate Women's Studies programme at Bangor began in January 1994. For women in particular it provided a unique chance to combine personal development with work and family commitments. The programme was set up through the vision and energy of Sandra Sherwood in the Centre for Continuing Education (now the Department of Lifelong Learning), with the support of individual colleagues from other departments: Shan Ashton, Charlotte Williams, Sandra Betts, Kathy Hopewell, Pam Michael, Julia Wardaugh and Lily Crowther.

Since 1994, approximately 80 women have studied on the Diploma/MA course. They are mainly professional women, of all ages, working across North Wales in a range of jobs. While many of them had a first degree, there are a number of women without previous experience of higher education who have successfully completed the course. For all of them, the Women's Studies course was transformational: "It has opened up a whole new way of thinking... I know now that I am capable of going out there and doing more or less what I want" (quoted in Mackie 1999 p50). Two years for the taught part of the course and a further year at least for the dissertation requires a sustained commitment, during which time many students also went through radical personal change. Sandra used to say that in each cohort there would be 'at least one birth, one marriage and one divorce.' In this respect, the feminist pedagogy employed in the course – where students share experiences, relating theory to personal life stories and receiving constructive criticism and support from tutors – is very important.

Creation and Recreation

Women's Studies came into existence in the late 1960s when women in the west began to realise we had been left out of knowledge. "Men had been the knowledge makers and they had validated their own knowledge – about us – by reference to each other" (Spender 1980 p15-16). Women were largely excluded from the creation of knowledge by the male-dominated academic system and its emphasis on positivist 'objective' scientific enquiry. Women's contribution to the world, in whatever area of life, was largely ignored. And when we were the topic of investigation, the findings perpetuated myth and prejudice against women, since, in fact, 'scientific enquiry' was influenced by male subjectivity. Women's ways of knowing, female subjectivity, the possibility of uncertainty, were discounted as serious tools for furthering intellectual understanding.

Women's Studies, then, attempts to redress the balance. It focuses on the experience and lives of women, not only uncovering what has been left untouched but also revisiting existing research or 'knowledge' to analyse it from a feminist perspective, to question it. What does it tell us about power relations between men and women in a patriarchal society? How does gender help to explain certain behaviours and processes which have been taken to be 'the norm' or 'natural'? Through this kind of analysis women have been able to redefine different areas of experience, developing our own meanings of the world and of words themselves (for example, renaming women's work at home or identifying rape as an act of aggression rather than 'natural' sexuality, see Worrell and Etaugh 1994).

This helps us to grow in self-confidence as we begin "to appreciate that the deficiencies are not in us but in the system that has excluded us." (Spender, op.cit.) Underpinning this process is the element of social activism, the promotion of societal change that characterised the women's movement and created the need for new ways of analysing the world around us. And, indeed, the intention is for feminist research to stimulate action and change within the public (and private) sphere, crossing boundaries and forging new alliances, emphasising collaboration rather than competition (see Daniel, 1996).

For these reasons, Women's Studies draws on all areas of academic enquiry and employs an interdisciplinary, holistic approach to learning and research. The programme at Bangor has three core modules. *Women's Issues* looks at gender in the family, the workplace, history, social policy and globally. *Feminist Theory* explores the different feminist perspectives (Liberal, Black, Lesbian, Psycho-analytic, Post-Modernist) which can inform the construction and deconstruction of knowledge. *Feminist Research Methods* aims to equip students with the tools to carry out their own research project within a feminist framework. There are a series of option modules from different disciplines which are taught by specialists: for example, Deviant Women; Welsh Women's History; Women, Work and Community; Women in Literature and Women, Film and Popular Culture. There are student exchanges with the School of Nursing (MSc in Health Promotion) and the School of Education (MEd) to broaden the range of options.

Finding a Voice
For most students at Masters level, writing a dissertation is a daunting task – and many on the Women's Studies programme see this as their greatest challenge and their greatest achievement. The selection of a topic is the first hurdle. In the end, most students chose something very close to their own experience - their workplace, their profession, their client group – and use this to explore how women's self identity, aspirations, roles and relationships are defined and circumscribed by patriarchy. A number of dissertations attempt to identify changes in women's lives: from the impact of world events such as war, through the effects of developments in public policy or new technology, to changes brought about by new personal circumstances – motherhood, the menopause or returning to study.

Feminist research employs ethnographic, qualitative methods, in particular in-depth interviews, focus groups and observation. Such methods raise several important ethical issues which students have to try and resolve. They have or develop close relationships with their respondents and this brings with it responsibility. One issue is the question of confidentiality: will my colleague be identifiable when I write up what she said? There is a concern to ensure that respondents remain subjects, not objects, in the research process. There is the fear of raising unrealistic expectations about being able to influence change as a result of the research. There is a danger of 'opening the floodgates' when talking about personal experience: how can I express sympathy without overstepping my role of researcher into that of counsellor?

It is not easy maintaining a balance between the subjective and the objective: students need to keep an overview, make comparisons, refer back to key questions and secondary sources. At the writing stage, they have to work hard at finding their own voice, while trying to fairly and adequately represent the voice of others. Many experience an uncomfortable tension between all these aspects of the feminist research process and what they perceive to be the constraints of the academic dissertation format – the masculine paradigm for the presentation of 'knowledge'. It has to be said that none of the tutors have quite solved this particular paradox. Fortunately the students help keep us alive to the danger that Women's Studies can easily become subsumed by the system that it was created to challenge.

Celebrating women's achievement
Because the dissertations are centred within the authors' own experiences and the immediate locality, together they provide a unique insight into the lives of women in North Wales, past and present. As such, they constitute a valuable resource, which we feel should be made more widely available, for the benefit and interest of local professionals, academics, other women – and men.

Publishing some of the outputs from the MA Women's Studies programme is a way of celebrating women's achievements, both those of the students and those of their respondents. In addition, this enables us to celebrate the life and work of Sandra Sherwood, former Director of the programme, who died of cancer in June 2001. She is sadly missed by all who knew her. The monograph series is one way of highlighting the positive impact and influence Sandra had on individual women (both colleagues and students), on academia and indeed, through this, on public life.

For this first series, we have selected dissertations from the 1994 cohort, who worked closely with Sandra in the early years of the programme. The series reflects a variety of topic and approach while being firmly located in Wales. All of them deal with some aspect of change and each of them has different strengths, exemplifying particular elements in feminist research. In order to present the work for a wider audience, a certain amount of editing has been necessary. This has mainly involved the task of reducing those sections relating to general feminist theory and feminist methodology in order to highlight the specific research questions, original research findings and implications of each dissertation. The voice of each writer has been retained.

The Changing Roles of Women Travellers

Irene Norman's research (1996-7) sought to provide an insight into the roles, functions and daily activities of women Travellers on a semi-legal site in North Wales and to convey something of the complexity of the taboos and rules of pollution which govern their lives. She wanted to see how far traditional roles were changing and what the impact of change might be. The study was particularly ambitious because, unlike most of her contemporaries, Irene chose to focus on a topic outside her own immediate experience. This involved gaining access to members of a socially excluded group and building relationships in order to gain their confidence. In addition, she was entering a different culture with its own norms. This meant she had to suspend judgement on certain attitudes and behaviour in order to be able to observe, discuss and record them. Irene's skill as a participant observer and her sensitive exploration of power relations are what distinguish this research. Her analysis highlights Traveller women as an oppressed group with strategies for survival within the larger community of Travellers, themselves an oppressed group with strategies for survival against a hostile 'settled' society.

Patricia Daniel
Series Editor

References

Daniel, P. 1996, *We Share the Same Struggle*, Bangor: Môn / Arfon Central America Group

Karl, M. 1995, *Women and empowerment: participation in decision-making*, London: Zed Books

Mackie, S. 1998, 'Women's Studies Students: Expectations and Experience', MA dissertation, University of Wales at Bangor

Spender, D. 1980, 'Learning to Create our own Knowledge' *Convergence* Vol 8 no 1.

Worrell, J. and Etaugh, C. 1994, 'Transforming Theory and Research with Women' *Psychology of Women* Vol 18.

Other titles in the series

Continuity and Change in Women's Lives in Gwynedd 1937-1947
Marian Gwyn (awarded 1997)

Educating Women – Re-Educating Men?
Julie Hanson-Williams (awarded 1998)

Nurse Training in Caernarfon and Anglesey Hospital 1939-1945
Katherine Williams (awarded 2000)

THE CHANGING ROLES OF WOMEN TRAVELLERS

1. THE TRAVELLER WOMAN IN CONTEXT: AN OVERVIEW

This introduction aims to set the context by providing a brief historical overview of Gypsies[1] as a people with their own language, culture and traditions who have struggled to maintain their separate identity in the face of prejudice, oppression and ethnic cleansing. It seeks to give an insight into, and criticise some of the legislative practices, which seek the discontinuance of the tradition of a nomadic way of life.

It examines the concept of the stereotypical Gypsy woman and compares it with the reality, drawing on the literature which gives an insight into and highlights the strict codes of practice that govern Gypsy women's lives in a patriarchal culture. It also examines some of the effects of oppression, both generally and specifically in relation to Gypsy women, and sets out the reasons for undertaking this research, giving some background to the author's interest in Gypsy women and their lives.

There are estimated to be approximately 12,600 families in England and Wales (Department of the Environment 1994) who are defined or define themselves as Gypsies. Recognised as constituting a racial group for the purposes of the Race Relations Act 1976 and recognised as such by the judiciary since 1989 (C.R.E. v Dutton) gypsies have a long history of persecution, oppression and being the victims of supremist ideologies.

Gypsies, also known as Roma, Romani, Ludar and Roms, are a people who are close-knit and communal with a common cultural and linguistic heritage. They have a long history, tradition and culture and linguistic relationships between Indo-European dialects and the Romany language indicate that they originate from North West India although Okely (1985) disagrees with this theory. Reasons for their migrations, whether from India or not, vary but what is clear is that by the fifteenth century the appearance of a travelling people is documented in virtually every European country.

Contained within this is a history of mistreatment and tyranny: "The history of the Romany people is a story of relentless persecution. From the Middle Ages to the present day, they have been the target of racial discrimination and outright genocide" (Puxton 1978 p12). From their arrival in Europe they have been viewed as aliens maintaining their own traditions and cultural barriers between themselves and Gorgios (non-travelling people). The response this has provoked from the middle ages to present day is consistent persecution on a continuum from verbal racial abuse (Puxton 1978) to ethnic cleansing (Hawes and Perez 1995).

Fonseca (1995) indicates that this persecution crosses time, countries and class. In 1589 Denmark decreed the death penalty for being a Gypsy

---

[1] The terms Gypsy and Traveller will be used interchangeably throughout. This in no way indicates any racial or ethnic superiority. The term Traveller Gypsy will be used when it is the preferred term of a group or individual.

leader and fifty years later Sweden followed by instituting hanging as the punishment for being a male Gypsy. Bismarck in 1886 codified discrimination against native and foreign Gypsies encouraging persecution and the practice of ejection. Bounties were announced for the capture and/or death of Gypsies. Enslavement of gypsies in Rumania became accepted practice with complete abolition not occurring until 1864. Gypsies were the only racial group in addition to Jews to be identified for extermination during World War Two. The murder, often by being buried alive, of an estimated five hundred thousand gypsies took place during the fascist regime.

Since the war, attempts at destruction of the Gypsy nomadic tradition have continued with many countries passing legislation in an attempt to enforce assimilation-Poland in 1952, Czechoslovakia and Bulgaria in 1958, Britain in 1960 (Caravan Sites and Control of Development Act) and Romania in 1962. Other practices, particularly in former Eastern bloc countries have acquired a more covert approach, "such as the practice (particularly prevalent in eastern Slovakia) of sterilising women during hospital births and very often without their knowledge. Less underhand measures also continue, including the confiscation of Traveller children by Christian charities" (Fonseca 1995 p240)

The nomadic tradition and lifestyle, which is central to the lives of many gypsies, is often the linchpin on which prejudice and discriminatory practices appear to turn. A report from the Council of Europe states: "The fact that the Gypsy way of life is different from that of the total society has, unfortunately, caused many biased judgements on the Gypsies, and in many instances discrimination" (Wiklund 1969). Current legislative provision in the UK could be interpreted as a reflection of the prejudice attached to the Gypsy nomadic tradition. The Criminal Justice and Public Order Act 1994 appears to be diametrically opposed to the standpoint of the Council of Europe and the European Commission of Human Rights which is based on the ideals of actively defending and promoting the rights of Gypsies.

Following on from the Governments 1968 Caravans Act whose primary explicit aim was to alleviate the poverty and poor living conditions being experienced by many gypsy families, the Criminal Justice and Public Order Act has wide ranging implications for Gypsies. While the 1968 Act introduced a mandatory duty for Local Authorities to provide adequate accommodation for gypsies in their area, it also provided Authorities with additional powers to remove them from unauthorised land. Eric Lubbock M.P. addressing the House of Commons stated that "the stick is the Minister's direction and the carrot (represents) the much stronger powers, once sites have been made available, for the Local Authorities to move Gypsies from land they are occupying without permission" (House of Commons Debates 1968). The reality of this Act was that, by 1994, approximately one third of caravan dwellers still had no right of abode (Department of the Environment 1992).

This new Act not only abolishes the site provision duty of local authorities, but it makes the stationing of caravans on any highway, unoccupied ground, common land or land without the owners consent, a criminal offence. Additionally, the Act sets limits on the number of caravans which may congregate together, thus further endangering and oppressing Gypsy culture.

The Criminal Justice and Public Order Act which has received condemnation from The Commission for Racial Equality, civil rights groups and Save the Children emanates from a right wing, capitalist perspective and is to be criticised for a variety of reasons including its neglect of women's positions. Traveller women derive support, both emotional and physical from the extended family system. The limitation of the number of caravans will, if implemented, have the potential to impact on and damage this extended family structure. The Act, which is covertly aimed at assimilation and forcing Gypsies to adopt a settled existence, does not take into account the social isolation from peers and the discrimination from neighbours that Travellers experience when housed. It displays a lack of awareness of Gypsy women, whose lives are shaped by the family role and domestic responsibilities and who by virtue of their roles are often the main victims of discrimination.

Under the guise of empowering Gypsies to accept responsibility by encouraging them to provide for themselves through private provision (that is, purchasing of their own sites), the Act fails to take into account that when a planning application is made by Gypsies it is not granted in 90% of cases (see Sir David Mitchell in Hansard 1994). Kafkaesque in its thought processes, it has the powers to confiscate and sell trailers deemed to be illegally parked. Draconian in its edicts, the Act will, if fully implemented, not only further oppress and endanger the nomadic tradition of the Gypsy but will effectively criminalise a people for their ethnicity. Lord Irvine stated that *"the real effect of the legislation, which they dare not openly avow, is to make those who have no lawful place to reside in their vehicles disappear through the imposition of criminal sanctions"* (Hansard 1994). It is my belief that the Act constitutes legalised persecution of an oppressed race of people, which ultimately aims to ensure that the continuance of the nomadic tradition is so perilous and fraught with the risk of prosecution, that the settled existence is not the easiest but the only option left for British Travellers.

One classic response to oppression and oppressive systems of justice is a process of internalisation of the values of oppression, thus enabling a group to be simultaneously oppressed and oppressor. bell hooks (1991 p75), discussing the effects of racism on black men and its outcomes in terms of sexism and oppression of women, states: *"Assumptions that racism is more oppressing to black men than black women then and now are fundamentally based on acceptance of patriarchal notions of masculinity."* It is clear that in Gypsy culture this same acceptance of patriarchy is in place and one may argue that it has some of its roots in the racism and persecution Gypsies have been subjected to. The internalisation of an oppressor's value system, whether from a racist or sexist standpoint, can lead to a society where egalitarian relationships do not thrive. Cultural norms based on ideologies of supremacy, creating hierarchies which in turn oppress groups of people within that society, are often a product of oppression. In Gypsy culture there appears to be evidence to indicate that women exist within tightly defined norms which also make them the victims of oppression.

A series of diverse images of the "traditional" Gypsy, his wife and family are available for public consumption. Sibley (1995) comments on the resonance of both good and bad within these stereotypes. The good often represents a hankering for things lost, *"an unattainable fantasy, the bad real malign presence from which people want to distance themselves"* (Sibley 1995 p15). He discusses the concept that good stereotypes are often mentally situated in the past, romanticised, distant, having no current bearing on our present lives. He comments on the lack of perceptual congruity with the present day bad image - which is often dehumanised, anti-social and bestial.

Images of the quaint rural figure driving a horse-drawn caravan, living a simplistic life free from stress or paying tax, is certainly the enviable stereotype for many. But this figure is located firmly in the non-threatening past by virtue of the horse-drawn vehicle. Contemporary representations of the Gypsy as work-shy, criminal or socially parasitic, show that the image of the Gypsy male has another series of present day, negative stereotypes.

However if the male images are at best ill informed and at worst racist, the portrayal of Gypsy women in popular culture appears to represent female deviance, women of the "mad, bad or dangerous " categories with never a sacrificial virgin in sight. Heidensohn (1985), discussing these consistent representations of women in dualistic terms, describes them as, " *the saint and the scrubber*" (p108).

Consider the whore, the taunting flaunting woman with wild sexual proclivities dancing in firelight tempting "good" men, and the witch, the toothless hag telling fortunes, both familiar Gypsy stereotypes. Heidensohn considers these to be the two most powerful images of female deviance. These two images portray a lack of conformity, (and potential for freedom?) which challenges the traditional virtues good women are supposed to possess. Heidensohn states: *"It is my contention that the effect of many aspects of our culture is to produce conformity in women"* (p106). Patriarchally defined virtues, ascribed to women as "natural" qualities of a good woman include: sexual modesty and fidelity, highly developed maternal instincts, quiet contained behaviour and speech, the desire to look "nice". These are passive behaviour modes which will not challenge either macho behaviour or male supremacy. Indeed the stereotypical portrayal of Gypsy women is one that "decent" women, that is, women who have internalised patriarchal norms of idealised female stereotypes, will abhor as a disgrace.

Yet there is a huge gap between gendered stereotypical images of Gypsy women's behaviour and attitudes, and the reality. In Gypsy culture the women are recipients of an oppressive system which both regulates and controls their actions, bodies and sexuality. A rigid set of rules and taboos has traditionally governed and controlled the lives of Gypsy women providing prescribed standards of behaviour, dress codes and defining expectations. These rules have impacted on women's lives, dictating the way the live and perform many of their domestic tasks.

Vesy-Fitzgerald in *Gypsies of Britain* (1934) indicated the these rules included the posture women should adopt when sitting and bending, the way they behave in front of men and the way they perform many of their domestic duties. Nearly fifty years later, Okely (1983) found many of the taboos and rules still in place. The restrictive practices in relation to dress codes (modest clothing which should not expose the breasts, throat or legs) were discussed by Thompson in 1922 and appear not to have been greatly modified in contemporary practices. Okely found that the wearing of tight sweaters and hot pants was still banned, as was any article of clothing which displayed the women's bodies. The restrictions on posture, sitting and bending that both Thompson and Vesey-Fitzgerald discussed in the first half of the twentieth century, Okely found still to be in place fifty years later.

There exist for Gypsy women standards of modesty in relation to normal female functions, including menstruation, childbirth and breastfeeding, that in Gorgio terms would be considered excessive. The rituals and taboos in relation to menstruation are particularly strong, for example if a man slept with his wife and the sheets became stained by menstrual blood he would be considered unclean. Mary Douglas (1996) stated that such taboos were useful to assert male superiority. Underlying these rigid standards is a powerful belief in women's power to pollute the male. The women appear to approach the observance of many of these rules and taboos from a standpoint of accepting their own uncleanliness and the need for these rigid rulings to contain their ability to pollute. They therefore not only adhere to the rules but continue to reinforce and police them.

Early marriage is the norm for young women and, although not practised in all Gypsy families, there has long been a history of the groom paying a bride price to compensate the family for the loss of a daughter. This often resulted in young women being married to older men as they were in a better financial position than younger ones. Although monogamy now appears to be the norm, before World War 1 it was not unusual for a male to go through a form of marriage with the younger sisters of his wife if there were not enough available men for them to marry. This marriage could become permanent if no suitor was forthcoming or else the younger sister could move into a trailer thus establishing a new marriage if a suitable candidate appeared. The practice was however believed to have been continued among European Gypsies for a longer period (Thompson 1922).

Additional to these accepted rules in relation to modesty and pollution there are tightly prescribed modes of behaviour for women when mixing with Gorgio society. She is as clearly controlled and self-policed whether on or off home territory and the earnings she derives from her contacts with Gorgios appear to give her no real power within either her marriage or Gypsy culture. Her education and preparation for life has been solely within the context of a need to know and relevant only to her primary functions of wife and mother (Okely 1985).

However one must bear in mind that Thompson's work came very much from the perspective of "gentleman scholar" and his work is symptomatic of both its time and his patriarchal and colonial attitudes. While being radical for the period in adopting an anthropological approach, it nonetheless romanticises and carries with it the stamp of the English gentleman who appears to have a sense of patronage about "our" Gypsies. He must, however, be credited with work that was groundbreaking and still of value to current scholars, providing information about the pollution taboos and clues to their origins.

Okely was writing from the tradition of social anthropology and, as a feminist, is infinitely less patronising and willing to embrace the culture without making judgement. Her insights and knowledge, gained by her daily contacts while living with Gypsies, provides valuable information that is untainted by the patriarchal perspectives of Thompson. Her analysis of the pollution taboos are detailed and reveal much of the complexity of Traveller traditions. While providing a clear picture of life within the culture she is, as are all Gorgio writers, essentially a filter between the people and their voice. Ultimately we are left with her own analysis as opposed to their voice.

Fonseca (1995) writes from an almost journalistic yet romantic tradition in a book that is fascinating and enthralling, but lacks the analytical aspects of Okely. Fonseca's account of her time and travels with European Gypsies, while informative, is almost tangential in its approach, lacking the structure and format of Okely's work. She is more inclined to explore and give recognition to feelings, an area that Okely tends to skirt; again, the problem is of giving a voice.

The filter is less evident in *The Forgotton Lives, Gypsies and Travellers on the Westway Site* – an Ethnic Communities Oral History Project in London (1989). The Gypsies here have, to a large degree, their own voice. The book provides the opportunity for them to talk about their lives and experiences. Their stories were recorded on tape and then edited and transcribed by members the Project. Margaret, in describing her life, talks about her experiences of travelling, working in a chocolate factory and how sites are always placed where no Gorgio would like to live. She says: *"It's hard being a woman, and especially a Travelling woman because if you're on the road you've got no electric, you have your generator in the evening all right, but everything else is done by hard graft."* (p7).

Winnie says:" *The good thing about being a Traveller? I suppose you can get up and leave and go wherever. We can leave school when we're ten or eleven, we don't have to go to college, we don't have to stay on to get A Levels we're OK Nothing really it's all the same, there's nothing good about being a Traveller"* (p 11).

An unnamed, fifty six year old Gypsy talks about her life: *"To tell you the truth I didn't go to school. In my day there was no such thing as school for Travelling people, but our father and mother teached us. They didn't give us any education but teached us our prayers, how to pray, confirmation,*

Holy Communion and all that. My father and mother done that for me, they all do that. There was no such thing as school in them days" (p 4).

In all the women's stories there seemed to be an acceptance of their roles and no expectation of anything different or better happening to them. However there are some indicators that a process of change is taking place in the lives of some Gypsy women. In North Wales for example, workers from the further education service and Women's Aid informed me that Gypsy women were beginning to use these services. These two, unconnected, pieces of information began for me a process of thought which was to lead to this research.

Four years ago I visited the former G.D.R. as part of a project which looked at the changes taking place in women's lives after the " Wall" had come down. Although not on my official schedule, I visited Buchenwald and became aware for the first time of some of the suffering Gypsies had endured. Even now I do not have words for this experience but the horrors of the place and the experiences of the Gypsies, the women in particular, stayed with me.

Hearing about the local Gypsy women stirred memories and reawakened interest. It appeared to be that the choices they had made, accessing Women's Aid and learning to read, were the choices of strong women. These seemed the choices of women who were making decisions for themselves about how they wanted to live their lives or who they wanted to be. Yet the little I knew or had read about Gypsies either confirmed the stereotypical images or suggested Gypsy women were the victims of a lifestyle where domestic violence was perhaps the norm and they lived a controlled and constrained existence. My own lack of knowledge and ethnocentric attitudes became evident and I felt the need to find out more.

Reflecting on my attitude and the information which could be interpreted as indicators of change I decided to base my research around gypsy women and their lives.

The research sets out to explore the lives of Gypsy women on a site in North Wales, examining whether the roles women play are changing, to explore the nature and effects of change in relation to restrictions on women and to consider whether women are experiencing a greater freedom. It is not intended to be an in-depth study of the intricate complexities of the Gypsy cultural heritage or its effects on a large number of women. It seeks rather to examine the traditional roles of a small number of women within Gypsy culture, to identify changes within their roles and to present a "snapshot" of their lives.

2. RESEARCH METHODOLOGY

The methodology used by the researcher in this context is mainly dictated by the subject matter, which requires sensitivity of approach and a respect for culture and tradition. The other factor is the author's wish to operate within an eclectic feminist framework. This entails drawing on feminist thought and principles to underpin the research without commitment to one specific ideology.

Travelling people have an oral tradition, their history and culture being and remaining largely unwritten by themselves. Literacy skills have had little or no value in Traveller existence. "The black talk", Gypsy terminology for writing as identified by Jarman and Jarman (1991), is often still viewed with suspicion as a tool of oppression used by Gorgios and as a threat to Gypsy culture. As Fonseca (1994) says, this presents a dilemma for those writing about a largely illiterate people. Although there is evidence of changing culture in relation to the acquisition of literacy skills as indicated by the First Romani Congress of the European Union which took place in May 1994, some of the Gypsies contacted in this research still regard the written word with deep suspicion and mistrust.

While not decrying in any way the merits of quantitative research and its particular strengths of producing data which is clearly defined and measurable, its use in this instance would be inappropriate. As a methodology it is incompatible to the purposes of this research and insensitive to the Gypsy oral tradition. From the perspective of the desired outcomes it could both deprive the results of richness and narrow the responses.

The possibility of the researcher issuing questionnaires or reading and transcribing the answers to a set of formal questions could erect huge barriers thus engendering mistrust and incurring suspicion which could endanger the research to a degree which would make it unfeasible. The gaining of physical access to a site/sites is difficult enough, but the gaining of social access (Hornsby-Smith 1995) is a matter of prime importance. Such access would be virtually impossible if one adopted these methods. Therefor in an area of research that requires utmost sensitivity and has the potential to be fraught with tensions which could endanger the clarity of the research the methodology chosen has to be sympathetic to these factors.

The selection of qualitative methodology, within the feminist standpoint of valuing individual experience, provides the researcher with the necessary framework and tools. It provides the opportunity to gather material relating to the individual's subjective experience and to undergo a voyage of discovery into the culture and social structures of a particular group. The researcher is able to adopt an ethnographic, interpretative and naturalistic approach with a certain reliance on an emergence of design within the theoretical and conceptual framework, which in this instance, is imperative. Robson describes the process as "*the intention to provide a rich "thick" description which interprets the experience of people in the group from their own perspectives*" (1993 p148).

Researching this area from a basis of generic feminist values and principles is an integral part of the process. Feminists, who have examined and challenged the traditional patriarchal norms in relation to the concept of objectivity within research, have equated it with masculinity, the creation of a largely male preserve (Keller 1985). The ideas of research requiring emotional and intellectual distancing to preserve objectivity is challenged by Fee (1983) who rejects the ideas that emotional and social commitment are contradictory to scientific rationality. Mies (1983), in outlining her criteria for feminist research, stated that it must use women's histories and be part of collective discussion with women. This focus on the valuing of personal lives and experiences underpins feminism and the feminist standpoint.

However, there is potential for contradiction in that many of the feminist models would not fit comfortably with a Gypsy identity - an identity which has been described as being built around tribal priorities defining the taboos and rituals which determine the lives of individuals, making them truly communitarian (Fonseca 1995). In the Gypsy culture, responsibility for childcare and the domestic burden does rest with the women, but on a shared basis with the extended family. Feminist arguments in relation to women's subordination being grounded in small family units could in fact be interpreted as an irrelevance in this context (Chodorow 1978).

Equally, if one considers the Marxist feminist approach, taking into account that the Gypsies are "truly communitarian", one could then consider the division of labour, the domestic role and women's capacity to earn within Gypsy culture. Women have often had an earning capacity which has matched or outweighed that of the men's. Money is earned by women through a variety of methods including selling lace, heather and pegs, sales of clothes given by Gorgios and fortune telling. The payment of a bride price to compensate for the loss of a daughter has been a traditional custom, which recognises the contribution women can make to the family income. However, this earning capacity does not appear to give her any real power or status within the context of her marriage (Okely 1983).

Similarly, should the research and its interpretation take place within a radical feminist framework one would need to view it from a perspective that, until heterosexual relations are truly egalitarian, female oppression will continue. This state is unlikely to be accomplished in a culture that sustains a belief that women have an innate ability to pollute the male and must therefor be contained by rigid taboos and codes of behaviour. The beliefs expressed by a radical feminist philosophy in relation to achieving sexual egalitarianism would be an alien concept in Gypsy culture and very possibly an irrelevance. The radical feminist approach to female sexuality in relation to the Gypsy belief in female pollution would seek to contextualise this from a perspective of patriarchal control. Arguments from a radical standpoint would state that women will never be men's equal either in economic, social or political terms until the sex class system has been destroyed.

However, there is no suggestion that feminist theories can or should only be used in relation to cultures or contexts which are sympathetic to feminist values. Merely that the differing ideological standpoints which are encapsulated within the overarching term of "feminism" make it inappropriate to treat feminism as one set of beliefs or ideals (Griffin

1989). Yet the validation and recognition of individual experience, particularly in women lives, is one which crosses the divides of the differing feminist ideologies. Therefore it was the intention of the author to approach this research from an eclectic feminist perspective, drawing on generic feminist ideals and principles.

Ethical considerations

While recognising and believing that feminist research in general should seek to raise consciousness and bring about change, I did not perceive that this was the role of this particular research. While seeking to establish a genuine two-way process of communication, it would be inappropriate to the people who had chosen to participate in this study, for the researcher to seek to instigate change.

However, realistically, it must be acknowledged that all research, all social interaction, does effect some change. But the aim should be non-exploitative and seek to minimise any potential negative spin-offs. Considering the complexity of Gypsy culture, traditions and taboos, it was important for this research to remain as pure and untouched by the researcher's own beliefs as possible. Equally, should the researcher's own ideals become overly apparent, one effect could be withdrawal by the agreed participants - either due to male pressure or a sense of personal discomfort with those ideals.

Although, from a feminist standpoint, the culture appears to be patriarchal and oppressive to women, it has to be contextualised within a recognition of the need to survive as a persecuted group. It was important to maintain a stance which was non-judgmental and to prevent neglecting subtleties and nuances that may need to be taken into account in developing an interpretation of research findings.

The ethical perspective of the researcher also includes the possibility that writings on or about Gypsies is in essence a denial of their voice, as it involves others speaking, on their behalf, through a medium which is both culturally alien and largely unacceptable to them. There are similarities to the denial of women's voices throughout the ages, when one considers how masculine theory and writing has defined and informed women's norms, roles, sexuality and sanity. This perspective had to inform the practice and interpretation of the research as did sensitivity to the cultural norms of Gypsies.

The avoidance of colonial attitudes or stances is imperative, as is an awareness that a degree of subjectivity will be subconsciously and insidiously present. Okely discusses experiences of fieldwork done, "*among people who with a history of colonial rule, or with vulnerable minority status, or subject to greater metropolitan control,*" and concludes that "*this political reality affected the nature of the encounter*" (1992 p24).

An added layer in the complexity of addressing this research from a specific feminist standpoint was the religious aspect. Many UK Gypsies, and certainly the women that this research is centred around, are Roman

Catholics. The Catholic Church takes control of a woman's reproductive rights and decisions. Rich (1976) claims that reproductive rights lie at the core of feminism, both in the sense of freedom from reproductive obligations and its recuperation of motherhood. Rich's ideals reflect the researcher's own beliefs. These are coupled with a dislike of orthodox Christianity as a tool of female oppression as discussed by Mary Daly in *Beyond God the Father* (1986). This perspective of the researcher's must in no way be allowed to impinge; a knowledge of one's values, beliefs and prejudices and an ability to place them 'outside' is essential.

The actual method used to collect data was developed with sensitivity and was influenced by the participants. Fonseca cites the best piece of advice she received prior to beginning her research with gypsies as, "*Never ask questions and don't wear short skirts*" (p 14). Her mentor, an unnamed anthropologist who had conducted research with Gypsies, continued: "*Asking is no way to get answers.*" Fonseca also states: "*Gypsies lie. They lie a lot*" (p 15). Her perception of this penchant for lying is that, while they do not lie to each other they lie to *Gadje*. On the whole this is without malice, tending to tell what they think you may want to hear as a way of pleasing or amusing you. While not wishing to detract from Fonseca's expertise or experiences, it could be thought this interpretation a little trite. Placed in the historical context of racism, prejudice and persecution lying, telling the *Gagje* what he or she wants to hear, could be perceived as a strategy for survival.

Given this cultural and gendered context, the approach was therefore a focused, non-directive interview concentrating on individual experience. The rationale for this approach is that it is designed primarily to allow viewpoints, feelings and memories to emerge. It is a mode of operation that seeks to empower the participants, placing them at the centre of the process by enabling them to lead discussion. Questions, if they are used, are mere prompts, to help memory move into past experiences, open and free from possible judgement. They should be enabling devices to assist links to be made between past and present experience, expectations and aspirations. And essentially they need to be participant-centred, allowing both a sharing and mutual ownership of the process.

Gaining Access
The gaining of physical access to an area that has often been considered closed (the Gypsy encampment) was a relatively easy process through the use of a good contact. A friend and past colleague was appointed by the Local Education Authority to act as Coordinator for Traveller Education. Her main area of work at that time was concentrated in an area where a legal and a semi-legal site offered accommodation for a number of Gypsy families.

The appointment, the first of its kind in the area, was a result of a number of contributory factors. The Authority had a commitment to Equal Opportunities, which in the Welsh perspective was considered quite radical. It demanded that each school and college give a named member of their staff responsibilities for equal opportunities and at Authority level appointed one full time Officer/Advisor overall with special responsibilities for multicultural issues. A later appointment was made to support this with a half time secondment for Gender (the author). A series of meetings were set up with the schools providing a forum for sharing and a process for identifying needs, including professional development.

Information brought to that forum began to indicate that many Gypsy children had, at best, patchy attendance at their schools. Adopting a holistic view to this seemed the best approach and work was begun to develop curriculum materials, which would value and celebrate Gypsy culture. Integrated into school Personal and Social Education programmes, it was hoped that this may bring about some shift in children's attitudes. Alongside this a series of professional development events, aimed at raising awareness and developing the skills of teachers, was provided. Underlying these strategies was the hope that, by creating a more pleasant and happy learning environment for the Gypsy children, attendance would begin to improve.

However, this did not address other issues such as the parental attitudes and concerns, which were obviously a contributory factor to the truancy rates. Although Educational Social Workers were assigned to all schools, the workload of many was increased by the presence, or absence, of Gypsy children. The parish priests in the area were also particularly concerned about the education of the children, as were local Councillors. The outcome of this was the decision to make an appointment for a Traveller Coordinator, to work with the Equal Opportunities team and to manage educational issues relating to Gypsies in the area.

The appointment proved to be a successful idea, not least because of the skills and personality of the appointee. She rapidly sought to build good relations with Gypsy families, networking, working closely with parish priests and raising European funding. Relationships of trust and mutual respect were established and in spite of tensions caused by changes in her job role under local Government reorganisations, those relations have largely been maintained. Her present role now includes governor training, equal opportunities and managing a small team of support tutors who work with the schools and Gypsy children. However she maintains strong links with the Traveller families, visiting when she has the chance and is still held in high esteem by many Gypsies. When approached with the request for assistance with this research she agreed to help with the process.

While admiring both Okely's and Fonseca's approaches and outcomes, the resources they were able to access were largely unavailable for this research. In reality both were in privileged positions in terms of time, finance and freedom from family responsibilities to be able to commit to undertaking their research. Not being able to make a similar commitment yet wishing to make it a valid experience while working within tight constraints, it was essential for me to find a middle way. I decided that firstly it was important that the participants be encouraged to self-select, as this would from the outset dispel some of the power dimension. I also felt it was important that the women who decided to participate should be allowed to decide the venue and timing of the first meeting and, in the light of that, any arrangements for future meetings. To this end it was agreed that Sue (all names used are pseudonyms) would, a few weeks in advance, mention to several of the women that she had a friend who was interested in Gypsy women's lives.

This information was obviously passed around and discussed on site as Trudy, Assistant Coordinator and a support tutor, was asked if she knew anything about this friend of Sue's. Trudy, while not party to the original discussions, had been briefed and had participated in several telephone conversations with me about the research and became the link person. She was able to explain that the research was nothing to do with the L.E.A. and was not an attempt to gain extra support or funds for Traveller education but was a piece of personal research. In this, there would be no payments or clearly visible benefits for the participants. There was some discussion that people writing about their lives from their own perspective could be a good idea, as often things that were written about Gypsies were untrue or unsympathetic.

Over the weeks, the idea of a woman coming to talk about Gypsy women's lives appeared to take hold. Trudy kept the issue alive by mentioning it occasionally and the women themselves brought it up several times. Eventually three women demanded to know when this person was going to be coming, as they were willing to meet and talk. Although this was a smaller number than I had originally hoped for, it was at least a beginning and subsequently I had the opportunity to meet more.

It was agreed that the first meeting should take place on the semi-legal site where all three participants lived. I was invited to one of the women's trailers along with the support tutor, who would introduce us to each other and remain with us for at least the first interview.

A number of site visits were made and meetings took place at other venues used by the Traveller women, including the local shopping complex and their evening class. The women were generous in their sharing and these meetings provided a surprisingly large amount of qualitative / ethnographic material. This is presented within a thematic framework below.

3. THE FIELDWORK EXPERIENCE

This section presents an introduction to the participants in the process, the fieldwork and the local context. It will seek to examine aspects of Traveller women's lives within the following themes: the physical and social organisation of the sites; women's work; the socialisation of children; travelling and education.

The Main Participants
The women introduced below are the ones who made the major contribution to this research and were central to the process. Others, women and children, who also informed this research did not play such

major roles and are therefore not named here although their contributions are included. All names have been changed.

Pat, about thirty five, mother of seven living children, four girls and three boys, married at approximately sixteen when carrying her first child. Husband an alcoholic. Parents and grandparents all Travellers, eldest child of a family of twelve, possibly thirteen.

Gaynor, younger twin sister of Pat, married at approximately sixteen, mother of three children, two boys and one girl, first child conceived after approximately eighteen months of marriage. Widowed following a car crash.

Sacha, twenty, single, living with her Traveller parents.

Gaynor (2), eighteen, eldest daughter of Pat, named for her Aunt, has learning difficulties, unmarried, living with her parents.

Janis, sixteen, second daughter of Pat, unmarried and living with her parents.

Sally Anne, fifteen, second daughter in a family of ten children (nine surviving) living at home with parents, a Traveller male and an Irish countrywoman.

The Local Context

> "People don't like us in this town, they put up signs saying " Gypsies Out" and things. They follow us in town. We can't go in pubs or anywhere, they just won't serve us." **Janis**

During the course of my research I visited two sites, one legal and the other classed as semi-legal. Although the ten-year lease had expired over a year ago, there existed a form of tacit permission from the Council to remain there, at least on a temporary basis, until some firm decisions about the future of the families using the site could be reached. Discussions about extending the legal site to accommodate some of the families were ongoing.

It was on the semi-legal site that the women who had agreed to talk to me were living. Driving, for the first time, to this site on a cold January morning, the hostility of local residents towards the Gypsies was apparent. Hand-made signs and posters had been erected along both the main road and approaching roads saying things like "No Gypsies Here." The support tutor who was driving me to the site explained that throughout the town and surrounding areas there was a lot of ill feeling towards the travelling community and its continued presence in the area.

Recently, she explained, a woman purporting to be a friend to the Gypsies, had gained their confidence and warned them about the dangers of being moved to the legal site which the Council were proposing to enlarge. She had discussed with them the dangers of relocation to the site stressing that their children would suffer not only from lead pollution but be in danger of traffic accidents from the heavy traffic as the site was next to an extremely busy main road. This information was causing the Gypsies to reconsider relocation to the other site. However, it later transpired that the woman was the founder of a local campaign, C.A.T.S.(Campaign Against Traveller Sites). She lived near to the legal site and thus was not offering honest brokerage but had a vested interest in preventing an increase in the number of families sited there.

There was no lack of awareness among the Travellers about the animosity of local residents: "*If we go to a supermarket, Sainsburys and the like, a big bloke in a suit will follow us all round the shop. People make comments about us and refuse us entry to pubs and places.*" There is also an acute awareness of the "problem" they represent to the Local Authority, the current uncertainty of their position on a semi-legal site and their very real fears of being relocated to an area which would be detrimental to their children's health. Certainly the experiences of siting other Travellers is not encouraging. Many sites are placed in areas where Gorgios would not consider living. Travellers located on the Westway site, for example, complain of lead pollution, noise, constant traffic and refuse being stored next to their site over weekend periods prior to disposal (Ethnic Communities Oral History Project 1989).

Physical and Social Organisation of the Sites

> "*Michael, my brother, takes fits and it's hard in the night hearing him and you can't get a light to give him his tablets.*" **Sally Anne**

I spent more time at the semi-legal site, visiting the legal site only once to call and collect a Gypsy male for night class. Although there were similarities in terms of site organisation, there were clearly visible differences in terms of facilities. Approaching the legal site via a made up road illuminated by electricity it was easy to see that facilities had been provided which were far superior to those on the semi legal site.

The approach to the legal site via a side road directly off the main road was carefully screened by fast growing fir trees. Whether the intention of this was to afford some privacy for the residents, to minimise traffic noise or to protect the eyes of passing motorists from being affronted was unclear. The site was surrounded by open metal fencing and at the entrance a building to accommodate the Warden's office and a gate. Next to this, a concreted area served as a children's playground.

The site was divided into plots. For every two plots a shared toilet and washing block, with mains water and sewage, had been built. The plots were neatly fenced and well spaced out providing the occupants with a degree of privacy and room to accommodate their trailers (a preferred Gypsy term for caravans) and other vehicles. Although not idyllic - the surrounding area was quite flooded, the site itself had massive puddles and the traffic noise was constant - in contrast to the other site the travellers' basic needs appeared better provided for.

University of Wales, Bangor • Women's Studies Monograph Series
The Changing Lives of Women Travellers • Irene Norman

The semi-legal site is set close to a large general hospital on the outskirts of the town. This is a semi rural area with the site backing onto fields with a stream running through and piebald horses placidly grazing. Unlike the legal site the area is not surfaced and the rough earth is continually ploughed up by a variety of vehicles leaving it a sea of mud with deep potholes and puddles. In the light of the ten year lease there appeared to be little evidence of provision for the site users to make it more than barely habitable.

Turning into the site, the entrance of which is dominated by a large heap of scrap metal contained by rough fencing and a small pen holding a young piebald pony, the poverty of resources becomes obvious. There is no proper fencing and pedestrian and vehicular access is through an old and decrepit wooden gate. The site is without benefit of electricity or drainage. No toilet blocks or washing facilities are provided here for the plots, all water has to be collected from a central point close to the entrance. This is provided by two cold water taps installed with a block of concrete underneath to stand containers on, apparently the only concession to basic human needs.

Talking with Sally Ann it became obvious the hardship this causes: "*It's dirty and muddy, look at me, I only put these clothes on clean to come out tonight and they got all splashed just getting into the car.*" The lack of proper toilet facilities obviously distressed her as did the lack of access to hot water: "*We have to go to the taps in all weathers, sometimes it's freezing. It's hard keeping clean and I hate washing in cold water.*" Standing talking with me, she looked fresh and clean, hair shining, wearing well-pressed, if mud-bespattered jeans and a clean top and jacket.

Her mother, she said, would remain on the site happily if only they would tarmac, provide toilet/washing blocks and electricity. Having had ten children, "*nine living*" it was hard for her mother, particularly with Michael being prone to night fits. She explained the cost of the diesel was too high to keep the generators running at nights and how frightening it was for her mother having lost one child.

The site was organised into plots, each one having some rough dividing partitions to separate it from its neighbour. The difference between this and Gorgio caravan sites for either residential or holiday purposes was striking and immediately apparent. The lack of any kind of green or garden area, the roughly constructed dividing partitions, the unmade surface, the lack of electricity, all contributed to an impression of starkness and poverty. Each plot was quite large and contained a variety of vehicles, some two or three trailer units, others two trailers, a car and a lorry, but rarely just one trailer. These plots appeared to be designed for extended families, living in one plot but in a variety of trailer units. The types and styles of the units varied greatly, some very modern and ornate with sparkling chrome decorations, other less ornate and obviously older. Many of the cars and lorries appeared to my untutored eye to be comparatively new and expensive, Mercedes lorries and powerful family saloon cars.

University of Wales, Bangor • Women's Studies Monograph Series
The Changing Lives of Women Travellers • Irene Norman

Recalling a conversation I had with a television cameraman who was filming some Traveller children for Save The Children Fund, I remembered him saying that the Travellers had specifically asked him not to include any of their cars in the footage. He felt that this was almost a "scam" - deceiving people about the poverty of their children yet driving BMW cars. However, put into context of a nomadic tradition, the ownership of a powerful and reliable vehicle is not a luxury as it would be perceived in Gorgio culture, but a necessity to provide for a continued (semi) nomadic existence.

When talking with Pat and Gaynor about how the site was organised and the number of trailers, they explained each family had its own fenced plot and all the vehicles on that plot belonged to that family. In Pat's case, the older trailer we were sitting in was "*for the big girls.*" She and her husband slept in the new trailer with the younger children, Bobby, two, and Martha, four. When I asked about where the two older boys slept, she explained that they slept in their aunt's trailer with her two "*big boys*". Gaynor's daughter slept in the "*big girls*" trailer with her cousins.

At this point it became obvious to me that this Traveller family differed from any I had read about. Yet this situation appeared to be the norm, not just for this families but all the families occupying this site. And although this arrangement of gender segregation was clearly an accepted norm, it was one which seemed to cause some unease in discussion. It would, I felt, be both counter-productive and almost indelicate to pursue further. Questions about what age one became a "big girl" (and was this to do with the onset of menstruation or other physical developments and if so was it connected with women's ability to pollute?) remained unasked and therefore unanswered.

What was clear in this instance was the sisters lived on the same site on different plots and ensured that very separate sleeping arrangements were in place for their adolescent children. It was also clear that neither Gaynor nor Pat wished to discuss the reasons for this and may have felt it an intrusion had I pressed the point. However, Pat did say that in the summer, when she intended to go travelling, that all the family would be together in the new trailer. By implication, all would then be sleeping under the same roof. She explained that when families went travelling it was always the custom to use the "*best*" trailers.

It is open to interpretation whether the function of segregating the adolescents was primarily to provide the parents with some privacy by enabling them to sleep together in a less crowded trailer. As an off shoot of this, perhaps it was feared that leaving the adolescent children of mixed sex to sleep under one roof could be inappropriate. It could also, in view of a belief system which fears the female ability to pollute, be a strategy to protect the young males against *mochadi* (becoming ritually unclean, polluted).

Equally, one could speculate, in the light of a history of persecution and the strong feelings of dislike and rejection which this group of Travellers are currently experiencing from the local population, that this practice is an act of self protection. It is unwise to arouse envy, and the owning of more than one trailer to live in could be perceived by some Gorgios as a conspicuous act of wealth which Travellers are not entitled to. One of the ways by which Travelling Gypsies have survived is to present themselves as poor and thus arouse no envy. Ownership of more than one "home" in Gorgio culture is associated with wealth and often power. However it is an accepted cultural norm among Gorgios that siblings of the same sex do not share sleeping accommodation after attaining adolescence. Thus it could be interpreted that, using this as a justification for owning more than one trailer unit, is one which Gorgios would be forced to understand and condone.

It could be argued that this is a sophisticated or complex pattern of thought, a taking of Gorgio values and using them against them. However, persecuted people develop complex methods to ensure survival. And the request made to the cameraman, previously mentioned, not to film their cars demonstrates an awareness of Gorgio culture and values and a fear of arousing envy.

Women's Work

> *"It's so filthy living here with all this mud you have to do it (wash the carpets) twice a week, maybe more."* **Pat**

On the surface there was little to suggest that the lives of all the women I met, regardless of age or marital status, differed greatly from their grandmothers. Their lives seemed to be fairly narrow, dictated by the domestic responsibilities of cleaning, cooking and childcare. None of the women I talked with are currently involved in any work which brings financial gain, their days appear to revolve, and are structured, around servicing the needs of their families.

Tasks like fetching and carrying water, feeding fuel to stoves to heat water and warm trailers impose a heavy and time consuming domestic burden and are unchanged by the invention of labour-saving appliances. A washing machine requires mains water and a consistent power supply, as does a central heating system. A vacuum cleaner has little relevance if your power source is elbow grease and you have to clean your floors by first manually scrubbing then hanging out your carpets to dry while you wash the floor on your knees.

Mornings are dedicated to cleaning. This does not begin very early. The first time I visited the site I arrived at eleven thirty, by Traveller standards too early for visiting. I subsequently learned that Pat and her family had all got up extra early to ensure the trailer had been cleaned prior to my arrival. Gaynor had arrived early to help out with the domestic chores. The daily cleaning ritual includes washing all floors, windows and paintwork as well as general dusting, wiping work surfaces, washing up etc. Additionally all rugs, curtains and covers are washed at least twice a week. Cleaning the outside of the trailers, chrome, windows and paintwork is also included in the daily tasks, weather permitting. In addition to these tasks, laundering and ironing, often for a large family, must be accomplished.

Shopping is done on a daily basis. A lack of storage space and electricity to run fridges or freezers make the once a month big shop an impossibility for Traveller women. Afternoons are reserved for shopping. There appeared to be a sense of pride about knowing where to shop to obtain the best bargains which involved using different stores for certain commodities: *"Aldis is best for basics, you get cheap sugar and things there but Sainsburys is nicer food and more choice."* I was also recommended, for overall value for money and a good selection of items to try another supermarket chain sited on the far side of town whose own brand goods they endorsed.

Late afternoons, early evenings were for preparation and cooking of the main meal. Later there would be the washing up, cleaning round and the smaller children to get ready for bed.

This pattern is central to the women's lives and superficially it would appear that little had changed for these women from their grandmothers day. Yet looking deeper life has changed in several respects.

The women from this site do not have the additional burden of being required to earn which has always been a part of Traveller women's lives. Traditionally women would clean in the mornings, go *"calling"* in the afternoons (often selling the goods their men had made, pegs, baskets, wooden meat skewers) and purchase the food from their daily earnings, coming home to cook the family's evening meal. *Calling* for many women may have represented both a social as well as an economic activity, providing a temporary respite. Now it could appear that shopping has taken its place. The local out of town shopping complex certainly appears to be something of an informal rendezvous in the afternoons. Traveller women from both sites greet each other there and spend time catching up with news and gossip. There is a conspicuous absence of children on the shopping trips, it is the "big girls" who stay on site to care for them freeing their mothers to enjoy the experience unhindered by small children.

When the topic of shopping first came up I expressed sympathy with Pat and Gaynor about the difficulty of getting to the shops and the distance home carrying heavy bags. This earned me a look as if to query my intelligence, as if anyone would be so stupid as to walk that far when they could drive. Okely indicated that women did not drive and cites men not wishing their womenfolk to learn to drive as they would have too much independence: *"discouraging her from learning to drive a vehicle"* (Okely 1985 p205).

Gaynor drives but, to her evident disappointment and indignation, recently failed her test after driving for seven years. She appeared unsure whether she would bother with the test again: "As *I drive perfectly OK it is seems like a waste of money me trying again."* I wondered if it was Gaynor's status as a widow which made it acceptable for her to drive but this appeared not to be the case. Pat also drives and on a Sainsbury's expedition I observed several other Traveller women driving.

There appears little doubt that the freedom from being required to earn, and the ability to drive, have made a considerable difference to the women's workload. It has undoubtedly eased some of the burden that women have traditionally carried. However the primitive conditions of the site contribute to a heavy and laborious load which women still have to bear and one that their grandmothers would have no trouble identifying with.

Socialisation of Children

"We don't pet our Chavies (Children) and make 'em soft." **Pat**

Large families are traditional among Travellers and even today it is not unusual for there to be six or even ten children in one family. The number of children born to one family appears to have little to do with finance, whether they can afford it or not. Hawes and Perez (1996) state that *"this is often due to family and partner pressure rather than because of a preference of their own"* (p116). There is also the religious dimension to consider as most UK Travellers and certainly the ones I visited, are Roman Catholics. However, I witnessed a great fondness for children and the women obviously derived a lot of joy from them. Pat said she would like *"just one more"* but Gaynor, in the unlikely event of her remarrying, said that as her children were now teenagers she would not like any more.

There is a belief among Travellers that a large family is wealth, particularly when one grows old as close kin then accept responsibility for caring for the elderly of the family (Okely1985). It is also seen as central to a woman's life that she should bear children. Fonseca (1995) stated that she, being childless, frequently aroused the sympathies of Traveller women and that they viewed it as a tragedy that she appeared to be barren.

However prized and valued Traveller children are, they are not spoiled or pampered. They are expected from an early age to develop independence and self-reliance. As Pat said of Traveller children, *"they need to learn to stand on their own two feet and look after themselves."* Four year old Martha was sent out to play on the site with the expectation that she would get herself to the pick up point on time for when the mini bus arrived and see herself off to nursery school. Her mother explained that she had been devastated to miss the bus the previous week, crying all afternoon and would therefore be sure not miss it this week.

While there are generic skills of self-reliance that all the children are encouraged to develop, it is obvious that the girls and boys are the recipients of different and gendered learning experiences. The learning to *"stand on their own two feet"* when applied to girls applies mainly to the early acquisition of domestic skills. Pat, discussing her children's upbringing, said: *"We teach them to cook and clean from being young and to look after the others."* When asked if the boys learned similar skills, I was told: *"Boys can look out for the young ones on the site, all the big ones must do that but the boys have to help out the men."*

This appears to begin at a relatively early age. At the entrance to the site I watched men breaking scrap, assisted by two boys aged about four and seven. These children did not rush towards us asking questions and greeting us enthusiastically as children we had met in the early evening playing football had done. They were obviously not engaged in play, this morning it was time for work. Equipped with their own tools they were busily engaged on their own project of dismantling an old metal tea trolley. This was a task, separate from the men's, which was being tackled with a seriousness and determination that did not suggest fun. When I mentioned seeing the children, both Gaynor and Pat agreed that the boys would be helping the men. They explained that the older men and young boys remain on site to break and sort the scrap while the younger men went off site to collect it.

This division of labour appears to be just one aspect of the process of socialising children into distinct gender roles. Martha was being washed and dressed ready to go to nursery school. After washing her hands and face she then sat down to have her long hair brushed and curled. This intricate styling of her hair was obviously quite painful for the child as it seemed to involve lots of pulling and twisting of the strands into ringlets. When she cried out she was told that she would look pretty and it would be worth it to look like "*a real little girl*" when finished. Her attire, in a frilled denim dress, dainty patent shoes and white socks, could be considered to typify the image of a "*real little girl.*" Yet a more androgynous outfit of jeans, sweater and trainers would have not only been more suitable to the cold weather and muddy site but may have given her a less restricted range of play.

While watching Bobby, Pat's youngest son, being spruced up after his lunch, it was interesting to note how he was encouraged not to bawl with comments about being "*a little man.*" After being washed and brushed, he practised his nearly acquired skill of walking, tottering from one to the other to be told what "*a clever little man*" he was. Although not visibly spoiled, he was obviously well loved and all the compliments and discussions about his attributes had at the core his "manliness." His outfit echoed ones I had observed Traveller men wearing, white shirt, waistcoat, formal trousers, and a bow tie as opposed to a normal tie. No androdogyny here either, a real *little man's* outfit.

Discussing my observations later with a Traveller Support Tutor, I enquired if she had noticed any discernible differences when teaching Traveller children. Commenting that boys always tend to be more demanding in class and are often more difficult to manage, she felt that this was even truer of Traveller boys. This she felt reflected some of the cultural values placed on the boys to be men. She felt that their attitudes and behaviour could from a relatively early age be perceived as "*macho*" and their behaving in this way often "*created problems.*" She felt that this type of behaviour seemed to interfere with their learning, particularly with a woman teacher.

Her comments and experience were reminiscent of when I taught Afro-Caribbean youths in London. Their culture too values masculinity and their boy children are often praised for displaying macho behaviour. To succeed with their learning it was always important to create a culture in the classroom where they felt respected for their masculinity.

There can be little doubt that the socialisation of Traveller children is gender biased and does perpetuate sexist attitudes. The sexist and oppressive culture that Traveller women live within has to be due to some extent to this process. However, for the mothers who perpetuate this with their daughters it is an act of love - to make them acceptable as wives within their own society which offers no other role but wife and motherhood.

Travelling

> "Coventry, Birmingham, by the canals, we travelled a lot as chavies." **Gaynor**

Being driven by the need to travel is a quality that many Travellers perceive as genetic, a way of defining one's self or establishing status. "*I suppose we've been Travellers all our lives, our parents was Travellers all their lives so that's it.*" "*When you're travelling you want to keep travelling, I know for a fact you cannot settle in a house.*" "*I was born in a tent on the side of the road*" (Gypsies and Travellers on the Westway Site 1989 pages 2, 15 & 16).

Yet according to Okely, being housed or settled on one site does not represent a loss of Traveller identity. "*The birthright is retained by children of Gypsies who have moved into houses as long as they associate with other Gypsies. A young woman explained to me "They are still called Travellers if they keep in touch with Travellers*" (1985 p130).

Discussing travelling with both the older and younger women, there emerged somewhat different pictures. Gaynor and Pat both reminisced fondly about their childhood travels with their parents. For them in their childhood and teenage years it seemed there had been a lot of pleasure in travelling. Pat explained that as soon as she was married she moved into his trailer with her husband and they set off travelling. Looking back she seemed a little awed at herself: "*There I was, a kid really and pregnant and we just went off.*"

Although both spoke with strong Irish accents, they had no recollection of ever travelling through Ireland. It seemed that most of their memories were of the Midlands, Coventry, Stoke and the Potteries. Their parents and many of their fellow Travellers had originated in Ireland yet seemed to contain their travels to this area.

Pat, after several years of marriage, did "*settle to a house*" and lived there for about three years until she happily took to the road again. She had been on the site now for about eight years, her sister joining her there a year later. Gaynor currently had no desire to travel; this was not based on her widowhood but rather her health, which she said was poor. She liked the idea of being sited next to the hospital as she suffered from a variety of ailments and found comfort in its proximity.

Pat, on the other hand, explained that she had every intention of travelling this summer in the new trailer I had doubtless noticed outside. Janis, Pat told me, had returned to the trailer the previous evening after spending some time travelling with relatives in the Midlands. She was grumpy and uncommunicative at this point, saying nothing about her experiences - only that she was tired by the lateness of the hour she returned home.

Later talking with her and Sally Ann, it emerged that Janis was not overly impressed with the lifestyle. Whether she had not wished to distress her mother by her lack of enthusiasm or was afraid of appearing disloyal in front of me she did not explain. However it was apparent from the little she said that she did not relish the prospect of spending the summer travelling. Sally Anne, always the more open of the two, was quick to articulate her feelings about travelling. She had clear memories of travelling a lot as a small child and how the family became tired of being constantly moved on.

> *"There is nowhere to travel to now anyway, Deeside? Queensferry? The gavvers (Police) just come at six, seven in the morning, get you out of bed and make you go. They say things like 'Its not us luv it's the Council they want you shifted' but it doesn't matter who, you still get shifted all the same. I hate it, it's frightening when you're asleep and someone comes round banging and shouting."*

Maybe Pat and Gaynor had romanticised their memories of travelling, remembering only the good sites, the companionship of the road, fine weather and feelings of freedom or maybe that had been the reality of their experience. However it was clear that for the younger women that their experiences had been different and time for them had not added any rosy glow to colour their memories. The increase in traffic, their experiences with the police, the lack of places to go were leading them to decide that for them travelling did not represent a lifestyle to aspire to.

However, what was clear in both the young and older women's statements was a strong sense of self-identification as a Travelling Gypsy (Pat's preferred terminology). There was no rejection of ethnicity in the rejection of the actual travelling and the desires for a more settled existence. A tentative question - inferring that if they no longer travelled were they then no longer Travellers - brought sympathy for my ignorance and lack of understanding. It was to them as incomprehensible as me saying I was no longer Welsh during all the years I lived in England.

Education

> *"My mum can read and write and everything, she's a countrywoman so she went to school proper."*
> **Sally Anne**

Education Authorities on the whole have always had difficult and problematic relationships with Travellers. The value of a Gorgio education has always been questionable to a people who educate their children according to their own cultural and family needs. For a people whose tradition has been an oral one, learning to read and write has almost been an irrelevance. However, things are changing and the Travellers I met are all currently learning to read and write. This does not indicate a huge shift in Traveller attitude towards becoming literate or that the majority of UK Travellers are all eagerly accessing education. It is worth bearing in mind that I gained my access to this group of Travellers via the education service.

The classes that the women attend began in a small way with an adult literacy tutor befriending several of the women and gaining their trust. She learned that two of the women wished to take driving tests and began giving free reading lessons in a trailer. As word got around that friendly and informal lessons were available on site more women began attending, until they required more space. Good relationships existed with the local parish priest and, with his support, classes then moved to the parish hall. All the women are Roman Catholic and felt safe about moving the class to this new venue. Later when confidence was established, the class moved to an outreach centre of the local college, which had better facilities.

Funding for this came to the college via the Welsh Funding Council. Because the WFC mechanisms make it unviable to run small classes with a high level of tutor support, a joint bid was launched by the college and the L.E.A. to raise funding under the Family Literacy Scheme. Under the terms of the funding, this meant that the class could no longer be a woman-only group but must be extended to men and children. Although the aim of this is to widen participation, one effect has been that several of the women have ceased to attend class.

Pat and Gaynor have attended from the beginning. Gaynor received some schooling as a girl, albeit spasmodically due to the family travelling. Pat, however, as the eldest girl, had been usually kept at home to help and had received little in the way of education. As the class takes place two evenings a week, the older girls take it in turn to attend and baby-sit. With the exception of one teenager all have previously received some schooling, many leaving after joining secondary school. *"They don't teach you nothing, all they do is sit you in rows and make you read."* Janis continues to go to secondary school on an irregular basis and attends the night classes to help with her literacy skills. Sally Ann had ceased attending school at thirteen: *"I liked St Anne's* (primary school) *they taught us our prayers and they liked us there, big school was different. And we only had prayers in the mornings."*

Gaynor (2) attends the classes regularly. Although she has obvious learning disabilities she is now able, with great pride to write her own name unaided. Previously she attended the local school for children with learning disabilities and although she insists she enjoyed it, ceased to attend in her early teens. The school had been keen to encourage her to return, but Pat explained to me that *"she's big enough now not to go to school, her learning's here with us."*

All participants appeared to like the classes, the teenagers in particular. For them it seemed that being treated as an adult, the relaxed and informal classroom atmosphere, a curriculum that was sensitive to, and celebrated, Gypsy culture, all contributed to an enjoyable experience. And being able to eat sweets and crisps in class was an added bonus - making this a far cry from the education system they had rejected.

The women too were approving, not only of the night class but the nursery which had been opened for Traveller children. A bus, sponsored by the Save The Children Fund and staffed with a driver and helper, calls at the site to collect the under fives just before lunchtime to accommodate the late rising habits of the women. The children remain there for three hours, receiving a snack and drink during the session. This venture has proved popular not only with the mothers but also with the children.

The observed ambivalence towards the educational process can be interpreted in a positive way and it would appear that the system is working well from the Travellers' perspective. They are deciding for themselves what is relevant to them, they are taking from the system exactly what they require and effectively rejecting the rest. The nursery, with times structured to meet their personal schedules, enables them to complete their cleaning routines unhampered by small children. Children attending infant and primary schools are learning the basic skills of literacy and numeracy - skills which are now acquiring more currency in Traveller values. Secondary school is still largely being rejected, its curriculum perceived as irrelevant to Traveller needs. Additionally, the 'nine to four' timetable of school interferes with the work patterns of daily life, preventing the big girls from caring for the children in the afternoons. The adults and teenagers, having identified their own needs, are electing to acquire or improve reading and writing skills at the evening classes. These take place at a time which allows the women to prepare and serve the main meal - an important ritual. This opting in and out of the education system to meet their own needs is reflective of Traveller culture and may be one of the keys to how they have survived for so long as a persecuted group.

It is important to realise that the participants in this research are still victims of racist acts and the prejudiced views of the both the local and wider community. This has an impact which defines part of the Travellers' lives - their living conditions, their choice of places to shop, the reluctance of some to continue with the travelling tradition.

It is also apparent that while changes have taken place in their lives there is still a commitment to continuing many of the traditional roles for women. While there are obvious benefits for the women in discarding some of the traditional values, in particular relating to women driving, nonetheless there is still a strong commitment to maintaining others. The adherence to sustaining both their identities and the gendered status quo is a thread which runs through many of their conversations and is present in many aspects of their daily lives. Their taking from the education system what they require to meet their needs, the performance of their roles and domestic functions, the socialisation of their children, all speak of a separate and living culture.

4. MOTHERS AND DAUGHTERS

In this section I will focus more on the taboos, the concept of pollution and the influences on women's roles. I also aim to give voice to some of the younger participants in the research and to present some aspects of their lives, experiences and aspirations within that context.

> *"My Mother's ashamed, she's telling folk she's ill so she don't have to face 'em, that's why she wont talk to you."*
> **Sally Anne**

Throughout their lives all women play a variety of different and often complex roles. Daughter, wife, mother, sister, friend, each role brings with it different responsibilities, a code of behaviour and a set of expectations to which gender is central. For Traveller women there are added layers of complexity, some of which are due to the contradictory behaviours they are expected to display. Their girl children are given messages about their roles being domestic, secondary, passive and yet paradoxically they are also encouraged and valued for their fighting abilities. In their dealings with Gorgios, particularly when calling, a woman is expected to be outgoing, bold or even aggressive. At the same time she is *"hedged in by restriction, expected to be subservient to her husband and cautious with other men"* (Okely 1985 p 205).

The belief system in place in Gypsy culture in relation to *mochadi* - women's ability to pollute - and the constraints this places on women, adds another layer to that complexity. Fonseca (1995) clearly identifies that the belief in pollution and a fear of becoming *mochadi* is still strongly in existence today in European Traveller culture and echoes many of Okely's (1985) findings. The taboo against certain animals because of their perceived uncleanliness identified by Thompson (1922) is as clearly in place now among European Gypsies as it is among the Travellers I met with.

Sitting with Martha on my knee, drawing pictures to keep her amused while I talked with her mother and sisters, I saw she was clearly able to identify what my badly sketched pictures were meant to be. Excitedly naming the pig and horse she drew a blank at my, thoughtlessly drawn, cat. Her mother seeking to help her shuddered when she saw what I had drawn: *"Dirty filthy creatures we don't have any of them here,"* she said. The tutor leaning over to see the drawing suggested that it would be a good idea for the Travellers to get a few cats to keep the many rats who populated the site under control. Pat was clearly horrified at this suggestion and strongly reiterated her feelings about the intrinsic filth of cats.

The tension between the perceived inner cleanliness and the outer filth is believed to underlie the concept of pollution and a cat, licking it's own outer uncleanliness and thus polluting it's insides is grossly offensive and the epitome of filth to Travellers.

Pat's reaction to the cat and the way domestic tasks are performed indicate that some of the beliefs in pollution - and certain related taboos -

are still strongly in place. There was no sink in Pat's trailer, after drinking tea the cups were washed in a bowl and the water disposed of outside the trailer. Later when washing the children, a different bowl was used and the water once finished with was again quickly thrown outside.

The belief that a woman's sexuality has the power to pollute unless effectively constrained has been a strong tool in the oppression of women. However it appears there is some lessening of this among the women I met. The strictly prescribed dress codes which Okely (1985) cites as a mode of control, did not appear to operate. Fonseca (1995) also comments on the importance of modest dress, which does not emphasise women's bodies or sexuality in any way. However she also states that the European Travellers, although not allowed to breastfeed in front of their menfolk, do not objectify breasts as sexual in the same way that Gorgios do. She notes that the bra, when used, is not to enhance shape but is often the holder of the family bank - since this is where women keep their purses (a habit that Pat had).

The clothing of the women I met varied from figure-hugging leggings or jeans coupled with well-fitting jumpers to the occasional shapeless jumpers which did in fact conceal the top half of the figure effectively. None of this seemed to tie in with Okely's descriptions: *"Tight sweaters were banned. If trousers were worn by women, the hips and upper thighs had to be covered by a dress or a smock"* (1985 p207).

Similarly the restriction on women's movements, bending from the waist, the keeping of legs together when sitting, were not apparent to me. Certainly Pat sitting on top of a work-surface smoking, an activity in previous times limited to post menopausal women, dressed in tight leggings and a figure hugging jumper, legs apart swinging her booted foot as she spoke, did not indicate that the restrictions identified by Okely had any relevance in her life.

The fact that none of the women I met were economically active in ways that bought them into daily contact with Gorgios may offer some explanation for a lessening of restrictive practices. Traditionally women have acted as an interface between the clean world of their own and the unclean world of the Gorgio. The functions that Traveller women perform when economically active, calling or trading with Gorgios, bring them into enforced regular contact with the external and foreign Gorgio environment. This contact represents an additional danger of women polluting and making ritually unclean her spouse or even the whole group. As women obtain, prepare and cook food the potential for pollution here is strong. The strict controls of a woman's behaviour and dress are partly aimed at ensuring she does not trade food for sexual favours, an act which according to Okely could *"threaten the ethnic inheritance of the group"* (1985 p207).

However the pollution beliefs of Travellers are notoriously difficult to assess accurately. Acton (1971) suggests that the belief identified by Thompson (1922) as regards woman's basic uncleanliness, has largely disappeared. An argument that Okely disputes while acknowledging that it was difficult to obtain definite confirmation. The subject is sensitive and the researcher is largely left to interpret findings in the light of her/his own knowledge and experiences.

Okely states that many Traveller women choose hospital births as an effective way of avoiding the huge danger of pollution that childbirth carries with it. Pat and Gaynor both chose to give birth to all of their children in hospitals and one could easily infer that this was their way of managing the danger of pollution that childbirth represents. Certainly in the light of Fonseca's (1995) work, childbirth is still considered, in the European context, to have the ability to pollute. She describes visiting a new mother who, along with her baby, was kept separate for forty days, being cared for among the older, post-menopausal, women. Other women were allowed to visit, although not if they were menstruating - as an added precaution against pollution. Men, including the father, would not be allowed to see the mother or child until the prescribed forty days had elapsed.

However, nothing Pat or Gaynor said indicated that their reasons for selecting hospital births were remotely to do with pollution. They appeared to express their preference on the grounds that it was a vast improvement on their mothers' experiences of childbirth: *"Asprin and pop was all our mother had to help her with the pains. Pop and asprin, wouldn't like to give birth with just them to help. Hospital is better."* Their attitudes seemed to infer that they were modern women availing themselves of the best painkilling drugs and medical care and their mothers' experiences belonged to the dark ages. Both of them had undergone Caesarean births on two occasions, which had reinforced their belief in hospitals being the right place to give birth.

The discussion on childbirth took place in the presence of two of Pat's teenage daughters, with no apparent embarrassment. It moved on to discussing the best pain reliever for period pains. *"Port or Port and Brandy mixed"* was felt to be much *"better than old pop and asprin any time"*, obviously a standard family remedy for pain. Pat was also equally open about being pregnant when she got married. It is unclear whether Pat felt as relaxed about her pregnancy then as she obviously does now. However this was not told as a cautionary tale to her daughters but matter of factly, as a part of Pat's own story.

All of these things run contrary to Okely's findings about menstruation being a taboo subject and young women being examined to ensure their virginity had been preserved. From Pat's discussion it was clear that she felt no stigma attached to her pre-marital sexual relationship (which had taken place in 1980-81 - about the time Okely was involved in her research). However eighteen years had passed for Pat to develop a sense of ease about her pregnancy and this could be in the light of changing sexual norms. There does appear to be some relaxation of the strict sexual codes which have previously governed women's lives, changing dress codes, open discussions about menstruation and pre-marital pregnancy. However, whether these are indicators of fundamental change is difficult to measure with such a small group.

Talking with Sacha, who is now twenty and still living with her parents, I had the distinct impression of a young woman who was "saving" herself. She expressed the desire for children and her own trailer but made it very clear that this would be in the context of marriage. Although relatively old, by Traveller standards, for an unmarried girl and not as physically attractive as some of the other young women, it was clear that she was holding out for marriage and would not be prepared to settle for less.

With Sally Ann I received conflicting impressions. Sally Ann's mother had been one of the women who had originally volunteered to participate in my research. She had seemed particularly eager and I had felt disappointed that she had felt too unwell to participate in any of the meetings and now seemed reluctant to talk to me. Sharing an illicit cigarette in the lavatory at college during the evening class created a bond between Sally Ann and myself, two "naughty girls" together. She decided that she could trust me and wanted to talk about the reasons for her mother's decision not to meet me.

Her mother, she explained, was a Countrywoman (non-Traveller female) who had met her husband as a young woman in Ireland and left her family to travel with him. Gaining acceptance as a Traveller wife is important but not easy for a Countrywoman. However Ginny, Sally Anne's mother, had worked hard to gain acceptance and to a large degree achieved it. Her skills at reading and writing had given her some cachet with fellow Travellers, who turned to her for assistance with anything which required literacy. She had also won respect on the site as a mediator, a role Okely (1985) clearly identifies as one of the functions of Traveller women. Ginny was always called upon to represent the Traveller views to the media when disputes or protests hit the press. She would also be called on when council officials, social workers and other 'establishment' figures would come to the site. She had established good relations with personnel from the education service, often mediating over children's non-attendance at primary school. However, the respect she had earned over the years of her marriage she now felt to be threatened by the actions of her eldest daughter.

It appeared a young, married, and by all accounts, attractive man from America had befriended the family, gaining their trust. He had come to the U.K to trace his Irish origins and to meet family, a journey which had led him to Ginny. A relationship had developed over a period of time between him and Sally Anne's elder sister. This had been kept secret from the family until they had run away together.

Ginny was shocked and deeply distressed, according to Sally Ann, and missed her: *"She helped out a lot with the young ones and was good with Michael and his fits."* Ginny had been distraught when she discovered them missing, *"phoning round everywhere, the Midlands and everywhere. She just rang everyone to see if she was safe. My Mum can do that, you know she has a book of numbers and is good with the phone."* A sense of pride in her mother and her abilities was evident here in what Sally Ann said.

What also came across very clearly was the deep sense of shame that Ginny was experiencing. The shame caused by her daughter's elopement with a married man was compounded by her sense of failure as a Traveller wife. From what Sally Ann said, it was clear that her mother felt that she had lost some of her credibility as a Traveller by her daughter's actions. She appeared to feel it was a part of her role, specific to being a Traveller wife and mother, to both protect her daughter and to ensure her sexuality was controlled in a manner as befits a Traveller woman. The deep sense of shame she was experiencing over her daughter's elopement also appeared to be linked to the fact that she was a Countrywoman not a real Traveller. She felt that this fact would be seized upon by her neighbours and give them the opportunity to point this out.

Hence her sudden refusal to meet and talk with me. Previous to this she had obviously gained self-confidence and credibility in her role as a Traveller wife, even some status among her peers. The actions of her daughter it seemed had stripped her of her self esteem and as a result she felt unable to face people and was staying indoors telling people, including Travellers, that she was ill.

Sally Ann was clearly experiencing very mixed emotions about the situation. She was missing her big sister, whom she had been close to. Her personal workload had increased, a fact that did not seem to bother her unduly. She was obviously saddened by, and seemed to comprehend, with a maturity beyond her years, the pain her mother was experiencing. It appeared since her sister's departure she had become something of a confidante to her mother; she was gradually slipping into the role her elder sister had occupied and was enjoying the status that this brought. Her mother had discussed her feelings in relation to the role of a countrywoman in this situation and Sally Ann could understand and empathise with her mother's feelings. Maybe as child of mixed parentage she too had needed to strive to achieve respect and acceptance from her peers.

It was difficult to assess what constituted the worst "offence" by Ginny's daughter - being sexually active outside of wedlock, committing adultery or running away and effectively rejecting the Traveller lifestyle . In Ginny's eyes, in her role as a Traveller wife and mother, she had not ensured that her daughter's sexuality was properly controlled and therefore she had failed and was shamed by this failure.

For Sally Ann, in spite of her concern for her Mothers feelings, the whole episode was tinged with a sort of glamour and sense of romance: *"He's an American you know the bloke she ran off with. He came over here from America"* she reiterated. *"I don't know what will happen to her cos he's married but she could go to America."* Anxiety for her sister was tinged with a certain envy. Clearly she envisaged a life for her sister which promised a different reality to fetching water from outside taps in wintry weather, washing in cold water and scrambling in the dark for Michael's tablets when he had another fit.

Janis, a close friend of Sally Ann's, knew the whole story and shared with Sally Ann a sense of wonderment about the man being American, the sense of romance and the same tinge of envy. Asking them both, in a semi-serious way, how they saw their lives when they were "grown up," I was touched by the pain in Sally Ann's voice: *"Married to a Traveller with heaps of kids. There's nothing else for me really is there?"* When I enquired what they would really like, they both said "jobs", any kind it didn't matter, they just wanted to work. Secretly, they said, their reason for attending evening classes was to improve their employment prospects.

I knew Janis had been undertaking work experience when she had been attending school. This was in the nearby school for children with learning disabilities, which her elder sister had attended. The school had set up a hairdressing salon and cafe to provide some experience of a realistic work environment for its pupils while still offering a high level of support. Janis had been working in the cafe, serving food, clearing tables and said she had enjoyed it. She had felt the experience wasted, though, as she knew no one in the area would give them jobs: *"Us being Travellers like we'll never get any job round here."* She was aware that she had been placed at the school for her work experience because no employers in the town would be prepared to give her a chance.

Talking previously with her mother about the work experience and the types of tasks that Janis was ostensibly learning to perform - clear tables and wash up - Pat was ostensibly supportive. She offered comments encouraging Janis to attend – but, catching the wry smiles that she exchanged with Gaynor and the lift of her eyebrow, I was aware of a certain sense of irony in the proceedings and wondered if this performance was for the benefit of the tutor who has present.

Sally Ann agreed with Janis about wanting a real job, saying she would really like to become a solicitor. When I asked if she knew what a solicitor did, she replied, *"Yes they know about the law and they go to court and stand up for Travellers."* Both of the young women seemed aware of the hurdles that faced them if they were to get any kind of job - local prejudice, lack of academic skills, high levels of unemployment - yet neither had yet given up hope and stated their intention of continuing with the classes.

Talking about her sister's experiences with school, Janis explained her mother had called a family conference of female relatives to discuss the question of Gaynor (2) returning to school. It had been the decision of the women that, although she could benefit further from attending school, her place now was with the women. She was, in Pat's words, *"good with the cleaning".* It had been agreed that she could attend the evening class but that night she was absent - sharing with her younger sister, fourteen, the chores of washing up, putting the young ones to bed and baby-sitting. Both of the young women seemed to accept without question the roles of women and girls in relation to childcare, family responsibilities and the domestic burden. They had no perception that the sharing of the domestic responsibilities which often meant they forgo school was anything other than a part of their role as young women and that role required them to put the wider needs of the family before their own.

Neither Pat nor Gaynor were present on this particular evening; one of their sisters in the Midlands was ill and they had been visiting daily to help with her and offer support. It did not seem incongruous to either of the girls that these visits were made on a daily basis. This involved completing the morning rituals of cleaning before setting off and driving back in the dark at night in inclement weather.

To them it seemed perfectly logical that this level of family support was in place for the sister who was ill. The arguably more sensible approach of one sister remaining there while the other one cared for her family was apparently inconceivable. They felt that it would be wrong for one of them to stay away and that it was not a woman's place to be away from home overnight. This applied equally to Gaynor, who was not bound by a husband, as it did to Pat, who was. The prescribed codes of acceptable behaviour exist for all women and not just "owned" ones.

It appears that these Traveller women's lives are still governed by the needs of their culture and demands of their families, which cannot be easily separated out and which continue to be intrinsically oppressive and patriarchal in structure. The women's roles, although complex, are nevertheless clearly defined in terms of duties, responsibilities and appropriate modes of behaviour. The continued existence of taboos and belief in pollution may seem to have lessened but still influence many aspects of their lives.

Although the younger women are beginning, at least superficially, to question their current norms and explore other options, it seems that there is nonetheless an acceptance of what they see as their roles. This acquiescence appears to be in the absence of any really viable alternative. There is a poignancy about the younger women who, by experiencing more contact with the outside world, have seen different things to aspire to and yet, by virtue of who and what they are, are denied access. Maybe in their acquiescence there is an awareness that this is the only way to survive, a little longer.

5. CONCLUSION

What emerges from this research is a picture of some aspects of the lives of Traveller women in North Wales today. It presents images of their experiences, many of which indicate their commitment to maintaining and preserving a cultural identity that society has deemed unacceptable and sought to destroy. Within this cultural identity their roles are still prescribed by a patriarchal tradition reinforcing their second class status as women. They seem caught in a double bind, experiencing racism from the external world and sexism from within their own.

In the light of this research one could consider the consistency of prejudice against, and persecution of, Gypsies as making some contribution to the oppression of Gypsy women. While it is a simplistic argument to suggest that the oppression of Gypsy women is solely due to their status as a persecuted people it nonetheless appears as a contributory factor to both their historical and current positions. Okely argues: *"to protect themselves as a distinct group within a society that is always trying to destroy them, the Gypsies uphold specific ethnic boundaries. These are based on the principal of descent, the practice of self employment, a commitment to certain values, an ideology of travelling and pollution taboos"* (1985 p34).

There is a danger that Gypsy culture is perceived as written in tablets of stone and that it is an unchanging tradition which must remain. Yet, in practice, change and adaptation has always been a strategy for survival that the Gypsy has adopted. The acquisition of different skills - from carving wood to laying tarmac - the shift from horse drawn vehicles to motorised ones, the move from rural to urban places, have all signified the ability to adapt and make change work for their culture, taking from it what they require to suit their needs.

While it appears that the belief in some pollution taboos is in decline, others are still strictly observed. However, the research demonstrates that where changes have been wrought in women's lives, these can often be connected to the lessening of the tight controls which were linked to the taboos which controlled and defined women's roles.

The acquisition of driving skills has had a tremendous impact on their lives, giving women a degree of personal freedom and independence not previously experienced. It provides the means to visit distant sick relatives, the independence to physically access literacy classes off-site, and to exercise choice over where they shop. Other changes include allowing women the freedom to smoke - a habit only previously allowed to men and post-menopausal women (who did not possess the ability to pollute). There is also the change in women's dress code; the taboos which insisted on clothes, which concealed and diffused their womanhood and controlled their posture, appear to be no longer observed.

However, the research demonstrates that pollution beliefs in relation to the concept of inner cleanliness still has value and is retained within the domestic sphere - playing a significant part in women's lives. The women's roles and lives are still shaped by the need for carrying out the plethora of domestic tasks to present the high standards of domestic cleanliness demanded. For Traveller women, there is little doubt that the continued commitment to the ideology of travelling or living in trailers often represents a hard and difficult life. However there is nothing to indicate among the older women that they are unhappy with this lifestyle or would wish to abandon it. For them it seems the only changes they require are improvements to their site or a new purpose-built site with decent amenities.

But the younger women, the teenagers, are beginning to question and may not be as accepting of the life style as their mothers. Subjected to more outside influences provided by education and television, they are increasingly aware of other ways of being. They are also aware that their options are limited by the inherent prejudice and racism which is so often a part of their contacts with the Gorgio world. It may be seen that this not only causes them pain but it also, ironically, reinforces their role as Travellers. While mainstream society condemns Travellers for excluding themselves from Gorgio society, the opportunity to participate in it is also limited. Sally-Ann's ambition to obtain a job, other than as a Traveller wife, is paradoxically rendered almost unachievable by the attitudes of the local Gorgio.

It is evident that the socialisation the girls receive from early childhood is intrinsically sexist, reinforcing gender stereotyping and that this is perpetrated primarily by the mothers. This process, which appears to equip the young women for little other than being Traveller wives and mothers, is not an irrelevance since the majority of young women will ultimately fulfil those roles. This is due on one hand to their culture and socialisation but also to the lack of real alternatives which are effectively stifled by Gorgio society.

The nurturing processes and socialisation of girls is aimed, as is all good parenting, at equipping children with the necessary skills to survive as an adult. For Traveller children, regardless of gender, the world they ultimately experience off-site is one that is often cruel and hostile to them. Giving children a sense of self both in terms of ethnicity and clear roles and the skills to fulfil those roles enables self-esteem and confidence to develop. While it can be argued that their socialisation stifles aspiration and limits choice it needs to be seen in context; living in contact with a culture that is hostile, a sense of identity and pride in that identity is extremely important. To be sure of one's place within one's society, and to have value for the contribution one is making, enables the individual to feel secure. In the changing world of Travellers, this is a valuable gift that Traveller women seek to give their children.

There can be little doubt that Traveller women, in spite of experiencing change, still live within a culture which oppresses women and within this, knowingly or unknowingly, practise a degree of complicity in the perpetuation of patriarchal values and expectations in relation to their daughters. Viewed from an outsider's perspective, this may be considered unacceptable. The practice however seeks to ensure the continuance of a culture, tradition and a way of life that is constantly under threat. For if Gypsies are to continue to survive in an ever increasingly hostile environment it may be that the needs for their women's liberation must take second place to the group's survival.

In conclusion I must say there is much left unsaid and much left undone; this research has only skimmed the surface of a fascinating subject. I am left with a sense of envy for Fonseca and Okely who had time to experience more. For more there is, a rich and gripping story, part of which was so generously shared with me by the Traveller women I met. If there is merit in this work they share it. It is their lives I have been privileged to touch, as they have touched mine, more deeply than they will ever know.

Acknowledgements

The author would like to thank the Traveller women, without whom none of this could have been written; friends and former colleagues in the Education Authority for providing contacts and support; Dr Julia Wardaugh for her excellent supervision; Sandra Sherwood for devising, coordinating and fighting for the course, and her invaluable and constant encouragement; colleagues, fellow students and friends for their support and kindness; Anna, Phil, David and Jack for their love, encouragement and belief in me.

GLOSSARY OF TERMS USED

Bender	tent constructed around bent wood
Calling	working, earning by calling at people's houses
Chavy or Chavo	child
Countrywoman	woman of non-Gypsy origin
Gadje, Gorgio	person of non-Gypsy origin (also Gadjo)
Gavver	policeman
Mochadi	polluted or unclean
The Black Talk	writing
Trailer, trailer unit	caravan
Vardo	horse drawn Trailer

BIBLIOGRAPHY

Acton, T. 1974, *Gypsy Politics and Social Change*, London: Routledge.

Chodorow, N. 1978, *The Reproduction of Mothering: Psychoanalysis and the Sociology of Gender*, Berkley: University of California.

Daly, M. 1973, *Beyond God the Father*, London: The Womens Press Ltd.

Denfield, R. 1995, *The New Victorians*, London: Simon & Schuster.

Department of Environment, 1992, *Consultation Paper. Reform of the Caravan Sites Act 1968*, London: D/E

Department of Environment, 1994, *Circular 1/94*, London: H.M.S.O.

Douglas, M. 1966, *Purity and Danger*, London: Routledge.

Douglas, M. 1975, *Implicit Meanings, Essays in Anthropology*, London: Routledge.

Fee, E. 1983, 'Womens Nature and Scientific Objectivity,' In M.Lowe and R.Hubbard (eds), *Womans Nature in Rationalisations of Inequality*, Oxford: Pergamon

Fonseca, I. 1995, *Bury Me Standing. The Gypsies and their Journey*, London: Vintage.

Griffin, C. 1995, 'Feminism, social psychology and qualitative research', In *The Psychologist*, March.

Hawes, D & Perez, B. 1996, *The Gypsy and the State*, London: The Policy Press.

Hansard, 1994, *House of Commons Debates Official Report* 6th Series, Vol 241, cols 355-379

Ethnic Communities Oral History Project, 1989, *The Forgotton Lives Gypsies and Travellers on the Westway Site*, London: Ethnic Communities Oral History Project

Gmelch, S. 1987, *Nan: The Life of an Irish Travelling Woman*, London: Pan Books

Heidensohn, F. 1985, *Women and Culture*, London: MacMillan.

Hornsby Smith, M. 1995, 'Gaining Access', In N. Gilbert (ed), *Researching Social Life*, London: Sage.

Hooks, B. 1991, *Yearning race gender and cultural politics*, London: Turnaround.

Jarman, A.O.H. & Jarman, E. 1991, *The Welsh Gypsies*, Cardiff: University of Wales Press

Keller, E.F. 1985, *Reflections on Gender and Science*, New Haven: Yale University Press

Mies, M. 1983, 'Towards a methodology for feminist research', In Bowles, G. and R. Duelli Klein (eds.) *Theories of Women's Studies*, London: Routledge & Kegan Paul.

Okely, J. 1985, *Changing Cultures. The Traveller-Gypsies*. Cambridge: Cambridge University Press

Okely, J. 1995, 'Thinking Through Fieldwork', In A. Bryman & R.G. Burgess.(eds) *Analysing qualitative data*, London: Routledge.

Okely, J. & Callaway, H. 1992, *Anthropology & Autobiography*, London: Routledge.

Puxton, G. 1978, *Roma: Europe's Gypsies*, London: Minorities Rights Group.

Rich, A. 1976, *Of Woman Born: Motherhood as Experience and Institution*, New York: W.W. Norton.

Robson, C. 1991, Real World Research*, London: Blackwell.*

Rogers, C.R. 1945, 'The Non-directive Method as a Technique for Social Research', *American Journal of Sociology.*

Smart, C. 1984, *The Ties that Bind: Law, Marriage and the Reproduction of Patriarchal Relations*, London: Routledge & Kegan Paul.

Sibley, D. 1995, *Geographies of Exclusion*, London: Routledge.

Spender, D. & Sarah, E. 1992, *Learning to Lose. Sexism and Education*, London: The Womens Press Ltd.

Thompson, T.W. 1922, The Uncleanliness of Women among English Gypsies, *Journal of the Gypsy Lore Society*, Third series, Vol 1 (1-2): 15-13.

Vesey-Fitzgerald, B. 1944, *Gypsies of Britain*, London: Chapman and Hall Ltd.

Wiklund, D. 1969, The Position of Gypsies in Member States*, Strasbourg: Council of Europe.*

MA WOMEN'S STUDIES DISSERTATIONS

Bradley, Susan (2000) *The Teenage View. A Study of the teenage experiences and attitudes of three generations of women*

Carrison, Janet (2000) *The Experience of Female Probation Officers Working for a Patriarchal Probation Service*

Davies, Kay (2000) *Lone Motherhood versus Patriarchal Hysteria*

Gwyn, Marian (1997) *Continuity and Change in Women's Lives in Gwynedd 1937-1947*

Gallienne, Yvonne (2000) *The New Teenage Pregnancy Policies:Empowerment or Regulation?*

Grant, Mairwena (1997) *The Punishment of 18th Century Welsh Women Criminals*

Hanson-Williams, Julie (1998) *Educating Women – Re-educating Men?*

Huws, Sioned (2002) *Llafur Cariad neu Llafur Rhad? Sefyllfa Menywod sy'n gweithio'n rhan amser ym maes Dysgu Cymraeg i Oedolion*

Jones, Hillary (2000) *Women and their Experiences of the SSD: A Retrospective View of Their Mothering Practices*

Kelly, Sandra (1999) *Menopause: through the eyes of 9 women*

Kincaid, Gail (2000) *The Changing Role of the Secretary*

Liddall, Liz (1998) *Women's Experiences of Mental Health Services*

Mackie, Susan (1999) *Women's Studies Students: Expectations and Experience*

McGarry, Eleanor (2000) *Representation and Patriarchal Ideology in Gothic Romance and Contemporary Formulaic Fiction*

Norman, Irene (1997) *Changing Roles of Women Travellers*

Potter, Sheila (1997) *Women Entrepreneurs: Financial Sources and Support Mechanisms: A Study of Businesswomen in Wales*

Sion, Catrin (2000) *Women in the BBC: how they feel about employment, motherhood and the Corporation*

Thompson, Fiona (2001) *Exploring Lesbianism in the British Military*

Trevelyan-Jones, Sue (2000) *The First Step. Older Women Returning to Learn at Access to Further Education Level in a Community Context*

Tyldesley, Patsy (1999) *Lovely Nannies: an investigation into the genderisation of women in educare*

Williams, Katherine (2000) *Nurse Training in the Caernarfon and Anglesey Hospital 1935-49*